An Urban Educator's Journey of Hope

ANNE CLARK

Copyright 2018 – Anne Clark

All rights reserved. No part of this book may be used or reproduced by any means, graphic, electronic, or mechanical, including photocopying, recording, taping or by any information storage retrieval system without the written permission of the author except in the case of brief quotations embodied in critical articles and reviews.

ISBN 978-1-945169-20-5

Published in Partnership with
Your Choice Publications
1245 W Princess St
York, PA 17404
717-850-3538
www.YourChoiceFoundation.org

&

Orison Publishers, Inc.
PO Box 188
Grantham, PA 17027
717-731-1405
www.OrisonPublishers.com
Publish your book now, marsha@orisonpublishers.com

Dedication

This book is dedicated to the children of York, Pennsylvania, and beyond. To all the authentic educators who have dedicated their lives and love to the betterment of the next generation. To my Heavenly Father for filling my heart with purpose, empathy, and love for learning.

To my children for teaching me the true meaning of love. To my grandchildren, who fill me with joy. To my mother, who is walking through this journey with me. To my beloved friends, who hold me down and raise me up at the same time. To my one love, who healed my broken pieces. No journey would be worth taking if we did not have people to walk the road with us.

I have these friends who lift me up and hold me down at the same time. ~*A. Clark*

Messages of Hope From Leaders

"I opened my arms to you once, and that means I opened my heart to you and hope for blessings for you always."
~Nohemi Ortiz

Helping

Our

People through

Education
~Ivan Beatty

"Your dreams (the seed) lies just beneath the surface. Your Hope and Faith nourish it to break through the darkest of hours. Nourish it and watch it bloom."
~Faith Angela Holley

"There is a village waiting for us to be a part of it. Find your village! Share your gifts and talents and openly receive what others have to give and share with you."
~Shannon Conway-Garcia

"Hope will never let you down."
~Jason Querry

"Hope allows each person the opportunity to change the course of their future. Lean into hope and breathe hope in. For by embracing the essence of hope through God, our fullness is obtainable, thereby enhancing life." ~Lisa Kennedy

Healing

Overcoming

Preserving

Excelling

~Shawna Harrell

"I used to hope for certain things and specific results. I have learned that hope, for me, is directly tied to faith. I hope that whatever circumstances I am in, God is using it and me for good." ~Carla Christopher

"When the world says, 'Give up,' let hope whisper, 'Try one more time.'" ~Angie Garrison

These messages and many more can be found in the book, *Messages of Hope from York, Pennsylvania* and on the Facebook page Messages of Hope from York, Pennsylvania.

Contents

Introduction ix

Chapter 1: I Feel Small 5

Chapter 2: Broken Road to Building Bridges 10

Chapter 3: We Have to Be Better 15

Chapter 4: The Power of Words 17

Chapter 5: Rock Star Five 19

Chapter 6: The Whole Way Broken 20

Chapter 7: Don't Cosign Crazy 23

Chapter 8: Use Your Powers for Good 25

Chapter 9: Say it Loud, Say it Proud 27

Chapter 10: Hope 28

Introduction

I'm Anne Clark, an author, educator, and community leader. I started on this journey more than six years ago, when my mom became ill with cancer. She has since gone into remission. During the time I spent in California with my mom as she was receiving treatment, I learned a great deal about myself—some things I liked, and some things I didn't like. After returning to my beloved school, Lincoln Charter, I focused on changing the things about myself that I didn't like, and in doing so, I started to do some amazing work for children. The purpose of writing this book is to give hope to other educators and offer some practical advice they can use in their journeys of hope to improve their schools for the children, the staff, the families, and the community.

I grew up in the church and learned about religion. Now, I know less about religion and more about walking and talking in faith. I know that the work I am doing was meant for me to do, and the work you are doing was meant for you to do. I want parents, educators, administrators, and community leaders to know that our children need us now more than ever before to demonstrate love and acceptance.

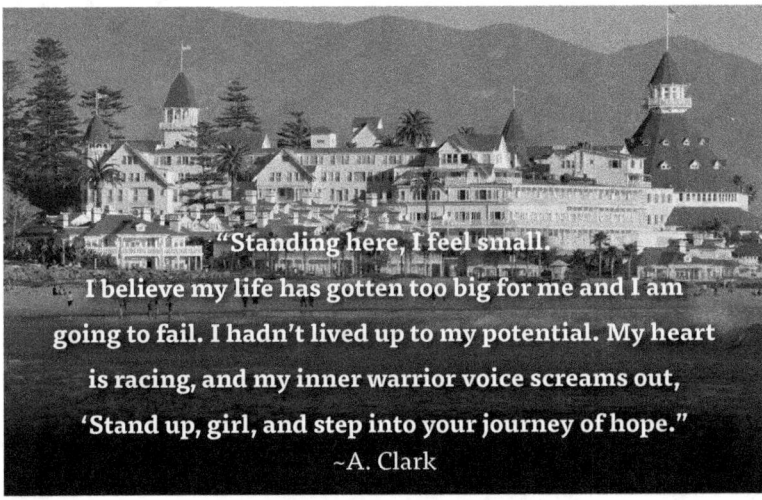

"Standing here, I feel small. I believe my life has gotten too big for me and I am going to fail. I hadn't lived up to my potential. My heart is racing, and my inner warrior voice screams out, 'Stand up, girl, and step into your journey of hope.'"
~A. Clark

Hotel Del Coronado, 2012

Chapter 1
I Feel Small

I sit now in the Hotel Del Coronado in California. I started this journey five years ago in this spot. My journey started here because, while standing in awe of this grand hotel on the Pacific coast, I realized that I felt small. That my life had gotten too big and I was afraid of failing. I realized that I had not lived up to my potential. My heart is racing; my inner warrior voice screams out, "Stand up, girl, and step into your purpose."

You may be wondering how an East Coast educator ended up here in California. The answer to that question and many others will come throughout the book. The purpose of this book is to bring hope to other educators, to parents, to children, and to communities. We authentic educators hold the power to turn our world around in less than twenty years if we commit to bringing hope to every classroom in the United States.

> **"Stop looking outside of yourself for the answers. You are the light and the hope of the next generation."** ~*A. Clark*

I thought about writing this first page for weeks prior to making this trip back to California, but I knew I could not put pen to paper until I was sitting right here at Hotel Del Coronado. I knew it was God's plan for me to begin the book where the story of hope began for me. I grew up in the Baptist church, which left most us of feeling guilty for being human. Now, I live in a space of spiritual awakening, and life is much easier, happier, and less stressful.

Be still, and know that I am God. I will be exalted among the nations;
I will be exalted in the earth! Psalm 46:10

In 2012, I received the worst call any child can receive from a parent. My heart literally stopped and broke at the same time as my mom spoke the words, "I have cancer." Without hesitation, I said, "I am coming to California." My mom was living in San Diego, but her treatment center was in Los Angeles. She would have to live there for two months.

On January 1, 2012, I boarded a plane and flew across the country. It was hard to leave my young adult children, leave work at Lincoln Charter School, and leave the community of York. However, that is what children do; they take care of their parents. This is true in many cultures. It is a duty, and we children are grateful to have the opportunity to give back to our parents.

"Hope is not a word; it is an action. It is a belief that my thoughts and behaviors can change the world." ~A. Clark

Just before I left on this journey of hope, my colleague Nohemi Ortiz and I met with a group of parents from the school. The moms were very upset that I would be gone from Lincoln Charter School for two months. I've learned from working in education for seventeen years that we are not only the teachers, principals, and support network for the children, but we also fill these same roles for many of the parents. Schools are unique places; we can be the extended family for our stakeholders, just as our colleagues can be extended families for us. In good schools, colleagues can be our best friends, our champions, and our teachers. Mrs. Ortiz is that type of colleague. She spoke the following words, and they still guide me daily: "Don't be sad for Ms. Clark. God has given her this opportunity to clear out of her life the people who do not support her."

I was incredibly moved by this and recognized immediately the truth in her words. God does give us opportunities to change the course of our lives. Most of us see the loss of a job or marriage as a failure. I challenge you to see it as an opportunity to take a broken-road experience and build a bridge with it—a bridge to a new future you.

Later that night, I spoke the same words to my children at our regular house meeting, which has been a family tradition since they were small. It still is the way we discuss the goals of the family unit. I added, "Pay attention to the people who help you while I am gone. Anyone we know who does not step forward, we are going to leave behind when this is over." Mrs. Ortiz was so wise, and her words changed my life. When I returned from California, my circle of friends and my children's circles of friends were cut in half. We were able to appreciate the people who stepped up, and we were able to separate from the people who stepped out.

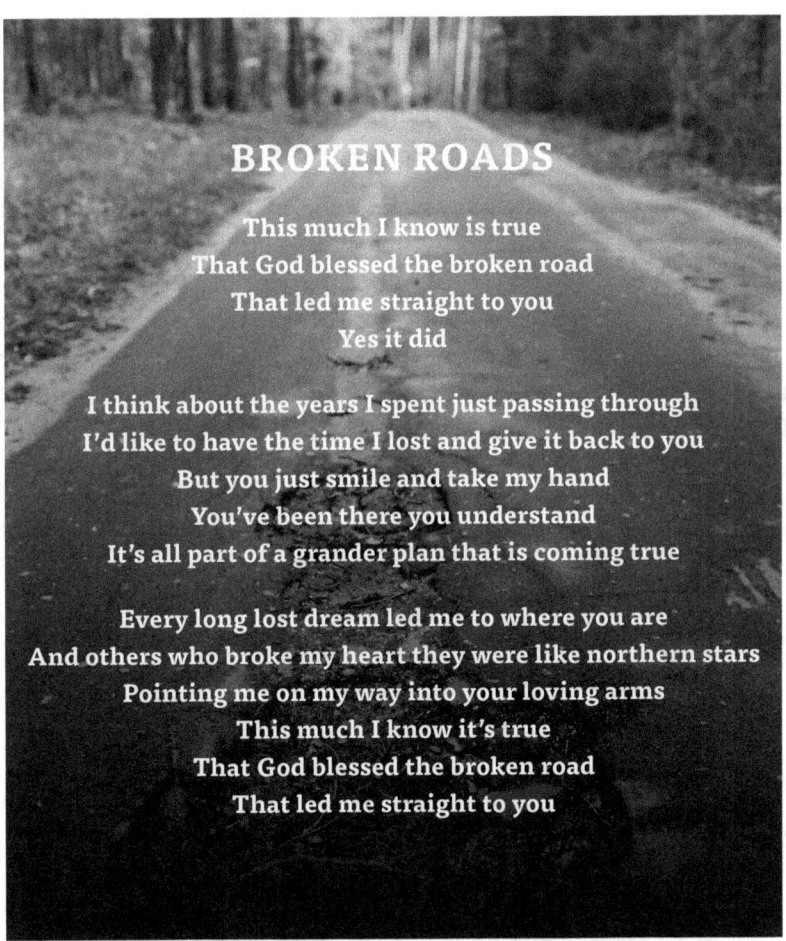

BROKEN ROADS

This much I know is true
That God blessed the broken road
That led me straight to you
Yes it did

I think about the years I spent just passing through
I'd like to have the time I lost and give it back to you
But you just smile and take my hand
You've been there you understand
It's all part of a grander plan that is coming true

Every long lost dream led me to where you are
And others who broke my heart they were like northern stars
Pointing me on my way into your loving arms
This much I know it's true
That God blessed the broken road
That led me straight to you

Songwriters: Jeff Hanna / Marcus Hummon / Robert E. Boyd
Bless the Broken Road lyrics © Universal Music Publishing Group, BMG Rights Management

At that time, my professional life was gaining momentum. I was leading a two-school initiative called "Road for Peace," an anti-bullying curriculum and program that we had designed from the ground up. I was leading the construction of our new playground with the help of AmeriHealth Mercy (now called AmeriHealth Caritas). The project was in its infancy. At the time, it seemed like the worst time to leave my job and travel to California. I now know it was the perfect time. It was God's time.

> *The heart of man plans his way, but the Lord establishes his steps.*
> *Proverbs 16:9*

"I'm traveling in fear and faith at the same time."
January 1, 2012 ~*A. Clark*

I arrived in LA, and my mom and brother met me at the airport. My mom looked terrible—weak and pale. She had lost the olive complexion that I'd always admired. I felt sad, the type of sadness that fills the core of your chest. That makes your body ache and makes it hard to breathe. I was praying for the strength to hold back tears and put on a smile. I found my childhood grit that had carried me through many hard times. This was the same grit you probably see in your students and feel in your heart—the determination to make the world better, even if it hurts while you're doing it.

When light comes through the darkness, there is hope.
~A. Clark

I had already come to terms with the fact that my mom's health was in God's hands. We were walking in downtown LA, and my head was spinning. I was looking for any sign from God that we were going to make it through this time.

I see the world more clearly through photographs. I am that person who takes pictures at the most awkward times. However, with that practice, I have caught images that change people's hearts. I couldn't have written this book and not included the pictures of my life.

"Fake it until you make it." ~ *A. Clark*

That day in Los Angeles, I looked up and saw light shining between the buildings. I felt then and still do that this was a sign from God. Much later, I had learned there is a scriptural passage explaining the same thing. I see God through images and repeated words.

> *The people walking in darkness have seen a great light; on those living in the land of deep darkness a light has dawned. Isaiah 9:2*

CHAPTER 2

Broken Road to Building Bridges

I want to give you background before going forward. I was born in 1966 in the York Hospital. My mom, Anastasia, comes from a small Greek family. My father, Jack, came from a large Spanish family, and he served in the Vietnam War. I was raised by my mother and my maternal grandfather, John Custis. My mother's mother, Anna, died of a stroke when I was three years old. I lived with her ghost for most of my childhood. People would say, "You are just like your grandma, Anna." I loved hearing that I was just like someone else. I was aware throughout my childhood that if my grandmother had lived, my childhood would have been much different.

John and Anna Custis in 1935 in York, Pennsylvania

> **"Know where you come from, but do not let it determine where you will end up."** ~ *A. Clark*

I grew up in great poverty. There was never any money for a want, and many times there wasn't even money for the needs. This experience instilled a hustle in me that I see in educators, business owners, athletes, and others who grew up in poverty. I see it many students who are living through the same poverty. Poverty made me want to work hard so I would never end up broke. I have spoken about this experience often with Dr. Leonard Hart, our principal at Lincoln Charter School. He had a similar experience as a child. We agree that if your background is impoverished, you never feel as if you have arrived. No matter what awards, accolades, or degrees you earn, there is always something else that needs to be accomplished.

> **"It's my job. No excuses."** ~ *A. Clark*

I have had five jobs since high school. I have stayed long enough at each one to learn all parts of a field before leaving. All of my past work experience has come into play as the director of community outreach for Lincoln Charter School. I love to work. I take great joy and pride in creating projects, programs, and strategies that make other people's lives easier. I have always loved the SMART work—the work that is specific, measurable, attainable, relevant, and timely. The work that joins human capital together.

I am a mother and *yaiyai* (grandmother). I have been successful as a mother, and I have been a failure as a mother. That is parenting. To me, it does not matter if you are a single parent or part of a unit, we all get things wrong and right. I've never let my failures be for nothing; I have sat across the table from many mothers and fathers over the years and stated, "I have been where you are sitting, and it gets better."

I became a mother at nineteen to my wonderful daughter and best friend, Tisha. She is now thirty-one years old and mother to my three grandchildren, Taliana, Dominic, and Avaiana. I also have three sons, Wayne, twenty-nine; Josh, twenty-seven; and Justin, twenty-five. Justin is going to be a father before this book goes to press. His son will be named Linken. I have a huge extended family, with stepchildren, students, and friends. I have been married and divorced twice. My second marriage was clearly what changed the course of my life.

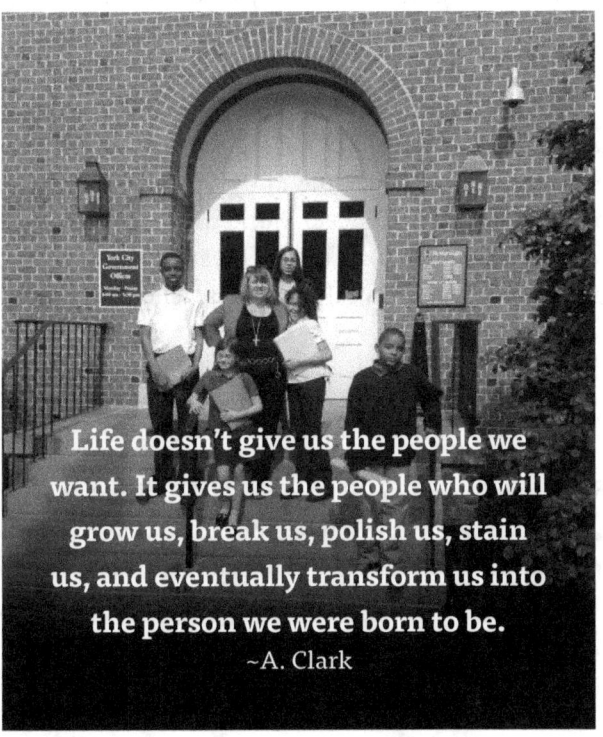

Life doesn't give us the people we want. It gives us the people who will grow us, break us, polish us, stain us, and eventually transform us into the person we were born to be.
~A. Clark

In 1997, I married, becoming Anne Clark, and over the next three years my entire world unraveled. Up until that point in my life, I had been fearless and strong. I had been independent and successful, and I had loved life as a single mother. I had great friends and a supportive family. I am still paying for that marriage in many ways and probably always will. My ex-husband was verbally and physically abusive. He abused my son, and I didn't know that until a few years ago. I will never forgive myself completely for that, and I believe that some things are meant to haunt us and keep us walking and living in purpose. That horrible marriage is what led me to Lincoln Charter School and my mission.

"I work for the children of York, Pennsylvania." ~*A. Clark*

In early August 2000, my husband asked me to return to work at our construction company. I had taken a break from the business to help my mother sort out my aunt's affairs. She had passed away not to long before this. I refused to return to the business. When you are in an abusive relationship, it may take many attempts to leave. He became very angry, he spoke the following words that changed my life: "You'll never find a job today." I was confident—more like desperate—to prove him wrong. I sat in my car thinking, where I am going to find a job? That little voice that we all have inside of us—that voice that I now know is the Holy Spirit—whispered, "The school district of the city of York." I'd never worked in any school, so this should not have been my plan. But as a child on Queens Street, when all the neighborhood kids played school, I was always the teacher. No one who knows me now would be surprised.

> *The Lord is close to the brokenhearted and saves those who are crushed in spirit. Psalm 38:14*

So, I went to the administration building and completed the application. The only job that was open was in the kitchen of the new charter school, and I was sent for an interview that very day. I did not want that job, and if I hadn't been so desperate, I would not have taken it. I had run a few companies, I owned a company, and that job felt beneath me. That is not my opinion today about any job in the school.

"Everyone works hard in a school, and everyone matters—from the janitor to the principal." ~A. Clark

The next day, I started the job. I know now that God was all over this. No one starts working at a school the day after she's interviewed. I tell people all the time that I grew up at Lincoln Charter School. I would encourage new educators to realize that they have not *arrived* just because they've been hired. Their time in education either will be very short, or it will last a lifetime. It depends on whether they allow themselves to grow. It also depends on whether they have the right mentors and the school offers the tools and support they need to grow in their capacities. The leader of a school is critical to the success of all staff.

I loved working in the kitchen at Lincoln Charter School. I loved the wonderful women, including the head cook, and the feeling of community. This community can be found in most kitchens. There is something about people who prepare food; they want to feed the souls of people around them.

This charter school had just opened a few weeks before I arrived. I knew nothing about what it meant to be a charter school, and now I am as close to an expert as anyone could be. It's funny that eighteen years later, part of my administrative work is serving as the director of the School Food Authority. In charter schools, everyone has multiple titles, and everyone works very hard.

I began to develop relationships with staff members beyond the kitchen. I could see that my organizational and coaching skills could be utilized to improve cafeteria procedures and the behavior of the students inside the cafeteria. I approached the principal, Mr. Fogle, about hiring me to run the cafeteria. To all the educators, I say, "Be the problem solver in the building, not the complainer." There are already plenty of complainers and not enough problem solvers.

By the following year, I was running the Lincoln Charter School cafeteria and working in the school office. I almost forgot; I'd also dumped the abusive husband.

Chapter 3
We Have to be Better

I'm so excited that I get paid to hang out with children all day that I'm tempted to pinch myself to know that it's real. They're so happy to see me every day. They smile, they hug, they high-five, and they tell me how beautiful I am. This is a great school full of wonderful children, and it's full of horrible adults. It doesn't take too long for the hater nation to emerge; I know all of you educators know exactly what I'm talking about. The haters are very loud, and they want any educator who wants to a make a school better to feel sad and small. I've heard everything over the last seventeen years, and let me state right now in this book that haters should hold no place in our educational system. They are toxic to the good work for many.

> *Do you not know that in a race all the runners run, but only one receives the prize? So run that you may obtain it. Every athlete exercises self-control in all things. They do it to receive a perishable wreath, but we an imperishable. 1 Corinthians 9:24–25*

As I would walk down the halls of Lincoln Charter School in the early days, I would shake my head and think, We have to be better than this. The way that some teachers speak to our urban children is criminal. I would think, Is this really our educational system? Children sitting in chairs for seven to eight hours a day, children on medication to get them to sit still, little to no recess, and the lowest of low expectations?

"We are educating for poverty, not for wealth." ~*A. Clark*

From the moment I arrived at Lincoln Charter School, I started to change the dialogue between adult and student. I wanted to model what authentic conversation can look like and show our children that they can respectfully disagree, and that they should be given their own voice. I decided that I would create the sweet spot of learning, where high expectations meet the right combination of tools and support, to change what holistic teaching looks like. It took Lincoln Charter School nearly twelve years to set criteria for being better. We did reach a higher level of student-to-teacher respect and success, but now it's time for the next level.

"You will never teach respect by being distrustful." ~ *A. Clark*

I want readers to be aware that we have over 49,000 failing schools in the United States. The structure of our schools is outdated for our students, parents, and teachers. The powers that be have been content to allow the blame game to continue, where parents believe school failure is due to the teachers, and teachers believe it is due to the parents. The reality is that those 49,000 failing schools are grossly underfunded, undermotivated, unadaptable, and poorly led. We need leaders who advocate the single message of success that we measure what matters and we are the inclusion centers of our communities.

"I was surrounded by the hopeless educators." ~ *A. Clark*

Schools like Lincoln Charter School are successful for many reasons, which include having the following attributes:

- They have a holistic approach to student learning that meets the academic, behavioral, and social needs of every child.

- They have created clear criteria for the school's four pillars, which include: mission, vision, tools, and support for stakeholders, especially teachers.

- They include parents and the community in the decision-making process.

CHAPTER 4
The Power of Words

In less than ten years, we could change our entire world by changing the words that we speak to our students and their parents and in our communities. Leaders, you must allow yourself time to be quiet and time to reflect on the words you use. I often tell students to use their powers for good, not evil. We need to give this message to our communities. I experience my whole world and all my relationships through the words spoken to me. Words give us the ability to build each other up or tear each other apart.

> "Your words matter, choose them wisely." ~ *A. Clark*

The Power of Teachers' Words
About ten years ago, during my teacher evaluation, my principal said, "Your words are transforming the children in your classroom from ordinary learners to extraordinary learners because of your positive praise." I then realized that this skill was unique to me and a few other educators. In the classrooms where teachers were speaking of student greatness, colleagues' greatness, and school greatness, student achievement went up.

A person's words can be life-giving water; words of true wisdom are as refreshing as a bubbling brook. Proverbs 18:4

In a classroom where the teacher has great control over tone, inflection, and the higher use of nonverbal communication, the children are calmer, and they reach a higher level of engagement and model the same skills as their teacher does.

The Power of Administrators' Words

People are going to talk in schools. The question is what they are going to talk about. This is where the leader has the greatest responsibility and the greatest power. Leaders need to have a clear mission and vision for their schools. Leaders need to demonstrate and be consistent in how information is disseminated to their teachers. Here are a few rules I live by when it comes to the power of words:

- See everyone as a student in your classroom; this will lighten your tone.

- Be clear and concise with your message; make three points and never speak for more than thirty minutes.

- Be positive; find the good in every stakeholder.

- Be the truth teller; if someone is wrong, you have to tell him or her.

- Give the big message to everyone at the same time; if it doesn't come from the leader, let it go.

- Do not entertain the slow-it-down questions; this is done by a select few to avoid the work or change.

- Celebrate your keepers of history; they'll help you avoid making the same mistakes as the last principal did.

- Believe that every suggestion can become to reality until it's proven that it can't.

"Build from what they know to what they need to know." ~ *A. Clark*

I have taken the power of my words one step further with Texting the Truth Sundays. It is so simple. I create a positive message, something from the heart, and I text it to twenty fellow leaders in my community. This practice has had a positive effect on my fellow leaders and on me. I started receiving messages back from my fellow leaders. I believed that these messages were so powerful that we created a book titled *Messages of Hope from York, Pennsylvania*. The book has 292 contributors and contains 343 uplifting messages. Our Facebook page attracted 4,000 members from forty counties in less than three months. We are now working on book two and have plans for book three. We hold the power to change our students, staff, and community outcomes with the power of our words. Be the speaker of truth, talent, and tenacity.

Chapter 5
Rock Star Five

A few years ago, while giving a presentation on the SMART Model to a group of educators, a participant asked, "Who helps you?"

I quickly replied, "My Rock Star Five." Your Rock Star Five are people who are experts on the project or initiative you are working on. There is no way to know everything; you are going to need other people to be successful. Now, I tell participants that the most critical part of the work on a new initiative or project is determining who your Rock Star Five are.

I have been a lifelong learner and have studied many areas, from technology to psychology. What I have learned about learning is that there is always more to learn. No matter how smart you are, there is always someone smarter. If you truly want to be successful, you will find the most qualified person to help you begin your project. The Rock Star Five you begin with may not be the Rock Star Five you end with. We need to celebrate the time people are with us and not feel badly when they leave us.

> *Iron sharpeneth iron; so a man sharpeneth the countenance of his friend.*
> *Proverbs 27:17*

When I pose the question, "Who is your Rock Star Five?" to many new leaders, they struggle to name five people other than their moms who are "rock stars" for them. This becomes the first step in their SMART work: creating authentic connections.

> **"Our moms are always our rock stars."** ~ *A. Clark*

Time plays such a huge role in our success and failure. I have seen many leaders fail with a new initiative or project because they want to do everything. Many times, think they know everything. The smartest people I have ever met waste no time faking what they don't know. Here are some suggestions that will help to find your Rock Star Five:

- Know your own mission.

- Look for people who share that mission.

- Speak your mission to everyone—and I mean *everyone* (develop a thirty-second "elevator pitch" describing your mission).

- Create a business card with your mission printed on it.

- Look for experts in all fields.

- Join an economic alliance or at least attend free events.

Chapter 6
The Whole Way Broken

How do you explain to people that you have been the whole way broken? How do you describe that deepest level of pain when your whole body aches? The type of pain that brings you to your knees and has your pray for mercy or death? The pain that leaves you no choice but to cry out for the Lord? I have had this pain in my life more than once. Sometimes it's been due to my own choices, and sometimes it's just been caused by life happening. Yet I have discovered that I am resilient. How do you explain the resilience of our urban leaders to our children?

I tell people sometimes that you have to get the whole way broken to get the whole way whole. My brokenness did not happen all at once. It had been building since I was a child. The breaks would come one at a time, and sometimes there were great periods between the breaks.

Trust in the Lord with all your heart, and do not lean on your own understanding. In all your ways acknowledge him, and he will make straight your paths. Proverbs 3:5–6

All my breaks came to a head in 2012, and I started to pray for my heart to be changed. I was really praying for God to make my heart hard so that I could not be hurt anymore. Be careful what you pray for, though, because God may give it to you. My gracious God created more situations where I experienced more pain, more ridicule, and more breaks. Through all the breaks, I became polished, forgiving, stronger, and more loving. My next book will be titled *Preparing for the Fall and the Rise*, inspired by our human capacity to love beyond reason and to rise each time we fall.

AN URBAN EDUCATOR'S JOURNEY OF HOPE

**I asked God to change my heart.
He gave me the ability to love more. ~*A. Clark***

I used to believe that every time I had a victory, a failure would come next. I would brace for the impact and try to get small. Like clockwork, someone would be there to point out every mistake that I had made. It made me feel incompetent, frustrated, and angry. I would react in anger, and that only created more isolation.

Sometimes we have to get the whole way broken, to get the whole way whole.
~A. Clark

Then I made the trip to California to be with my mom. It was the first time in my life that I was alone with me. For many long hours, I would sit outside the treatment center and have nothing to do but journal and think. The first two weeks were the worst: all I could think about were the mistakes I had made, and I had made a few. I had made mistakes in raising my children, in choosing a husband, in choosing friends, and by losing myself. I realized that I didn't know who I was as a person—not as a mother, or wife, or friend, or daughter, or employee. During weeks three and four, I came to the realization that I didn't like who I was. I was walking in fear! I wasn't afraid of failing; I was afraid of succeeding!

A few weeks later, the big, big, day arrived when God showed me exactly what walking in fear had earned me. My mother, brother, and I visited the historic Hotel Del Coronado. We approached from the beach, which is lined with multimillion-dollar beach homes. We stood at the edge of the ocean and looked at the grand hotel, and in that moment, I realized how small I was. Not because of my culture, not because of my parents, not because of education, or motivation, or work ethic, but because I had been walking in fear. That fear not only affected my work success, but it affected all areas of my life.

Hope Street Learning Lab Ribbon Cutting

In that moment, I realized that I can open any door. The attacks that I faced were not because of my success; the purpose of those attacks was for me to become polished, to grow my capacity to love and change my community. I was going to become the phoenix and rise with a fire never seen before in my school and my community. If I recognized any problem in my school or community, I was going to bring the answer to that problem. If students didn't have enough food, I would find food. If the students didn't have a place to play, I would create a playground. I could be the bringer of hope!

Chapter 7
Don't Cosign Crazy

Leadership demands that we tell the truth even when people do not want to hear it. It is never easy to tell people the truth, but it is necessary if you don't want your people to have a false sense of what is right and wrong. I have sat in leadership meetings in which the topic of toxic people has come up. I have experienced toxic people at all levels of the educational system, from parents to principal.

> *The LORD detests lying lips, but he delights in people who are trustworthy. Proverbs 12:22*

The toxic person will stay small if the leaders do not cosign on craziness. The negativity we experience in our schools can kill future success. A few years ago, I was sitting with one of our assistant principals on her last day at our school. I asked her why she was leaving now. She said, "I learned a lot about leadership from watching you this year. I learned leaders must be able to stand alone."

I replied, "I've learned to be my own best friend, because at the end of the day, I might be the only friend I have."

We had a challenging relationship over the years. I do credit her for the advice to change my major from child psychology to education. At that point in my career six years ago, I was working as the director of community outreach. My work was really hard because it was being done for the first time, and colleagues really didn't see the value in it. I felt that my assistant principal never defended my work or even stood up for me as a person. Those days at school were really lonely.

A few years after that conversation, I had the chance to sit with that assistant principal again. I asked her why she didn't speak up when she saw how I was being treated. She said that the relationships she had with people were more important to her than doing what was right.

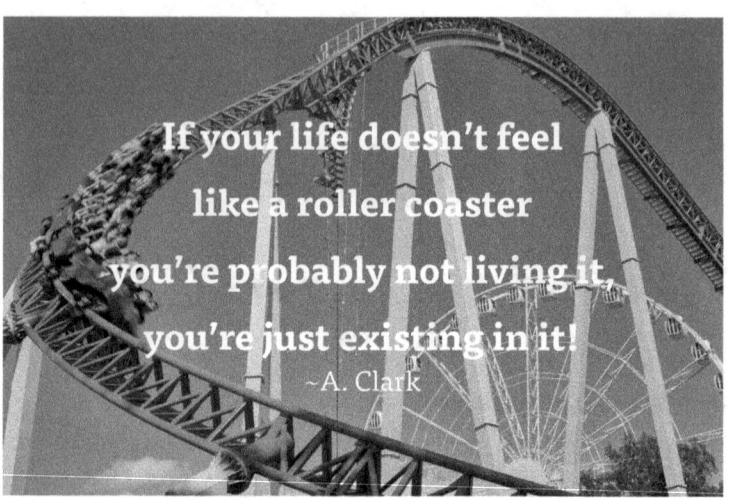

If your life doesn't feel like a roller coaster you're probably not living it, you're just existing in it!
~A. Clark

I know many of you are probably shaking your heads. However, she wasn't the only colleague to say that to me. I shared that fact with her. I also said that her silence made my colleagues believe that they were right in the things they said and in their treatment of others and me. I told her that her silence had been like "cosigning" or supporting the craziness of our toxic people, and it had slowed our success as an organization.

The authentic conversations of real American educators that are happening in the hallways of our schools needs to be happening in the PD trainings with our administrators and superintendents.
~A. Clark

I have been working through the truth model with students, parents, and colleagues for the last two years. In the truth model, the people in an organization realize the need to be speakers of truth at all levels—from students to parents to colleagues to community members. When people are stating untruths or have philosophies about peoples' situations that are not correct, everyone must stop them and say, "We don't do that here." Truth telling can become your culture and climate.

The Purpose of the Hater Nation

I also have learned that haters are sent by God to give us a chance to polish ourselves. I know now that haters will go after the project that has the most success and I need to be working harder on it. The haters come right before your victory. Start to look at your haters in this new framework, and your work will get even better. You may not always like the person who gives you the information you need, but you must take it anyway. I have realized that you can't listen to everyone, and yet you have to listen to someone. I have set clear criteria to determine who I will take advice from. I ask myself:

- Is the person smarter than I am?

- Is the person kinder than I am?

- Is the person living in greater purpose than I am?

If I answer yes to any of the above, I make myself listen and apply that person's suggestions. If I answer no to those questions, I wish the person well and move forward with my own thoughts. If you can answer all of your hater's questions and leave him or her speechless, you are ready for any audience and victory.

Chapter 8
Use Your Powers for Good

Once you are in a leadership role, you must use your powers for good. Many people think I am talking about adult leadership. But I believe leadership is demonstrated at all ages. I see these leadership qualities in children at all ages: when they tie each other's shoes, when they hold a friend's hand crossing a street, and when they stand up for a friend who is being bullied. The children are demonstrating one of the most important skills of leadership, which is "servant leadership"—putting others before ourselves.

> *But those who hope in the LORD will renew their strength. They will soar on wings like eagles; they will run and not grow weary, they will walk and not be faint. Isaiah 40:31*

I have counseled many children over the years and have spoken these words: "Use your powers for good." Even children in kindergarten understand that we have the ability to use our special powers to bring light, kindness, and friendship to others.

As educators, we must begin to see our roles as extending beyond the test, beyond reading, beyond math, even beyond writing to the whole child. Many times, the children in a classroom show us what they need in inappropriate ways. We lose our high-performing students to boredom, our quiet students to disruption, and our disruptive students to suspension.

We lose our high-performing students to boredom, our quiet students to disruption, and our disruptive students to suspension. ~ *A. Clark*

Anne Clark and members of Sigma Rho Sorority Inc. speak out at the March for Our Lives in York, Pennsylvania.

Our educational programs do not even come close to meeting the needs that we are facing in our communities. I believe this book will provide some practical knowledge to teachers. We all have our acronyms in the building, such as School Wide Behavioral System (SWEB). I do agree with having schoolwide structure and even programs to teach character education. However, what many schools are missing are empathy, love, and purpose for our students, their parents, and even other educators.

2018 Lincoln Charter School Ambassadors

Use Your Powers for Good

Lincoln Charter School ambassadors, Year 1

It is hard to give our students what they need when our faculty lacks tools, support, and fair funding in our inner cities. Change is possible even when we are operating with less. However, it will take you and your colleagues to send a clear message that:

- We can make change happen;
- I will be culturally competent;
- I will ask for help;
- I will partner with others; and
- I will use my powers for good.

Even when I was working without support of my immediate colleagues, which was the majority of the last eighteen years, I had authentic support from the parents and community leaders surrounding school. I also clearly spoke our Lion Pride: we are the lions, we are kind, and we serve our community. We are leaders and health champions, and we serve our community.

I want to end this chapter with the following thought: I couldn't have written this book six years ago. I was walking in fear of failure.

"You can't walk in fear and faith at the same time." ~*A. Clark*

Chapter 9

Say it Loud, Say it Proud

Picture in your mind halftime on any given Sunday at a Little League football game. Out in the center of the football field is a group of cheerleaders. Sometimes the only people in the stands are the parents because everyone else has gone to the snack stand. That little eight-year-old girl calling out to an empty stadium is not aware of the lack of a crowd. She is using her biggest little girl voice to scream out her team's battle call! That is passion! That is the type of passion that we must bring to the classroom and our assemblies for our students—and to our communities. Everyone around you will begin to want to join you. You will be the transformational leader that we need now!

Lincoln Charter School student lead a rally during Play Streets.

AN URBAN EDUCATOR'S JOURNEY OF HOPE

2017 Lincoln Charter School Ambassadors representing Hope Street Learning Lab.

That is why we labor and strive, because we have put our hope in the living God, who is the Savior of all people, and especially of those who believe. 1 Timothy 4:10

Your team is your students, your parents, your community, and your colleagues. Get them excited about where you want to go. However, be prepared to start the journey on your own. When I first wanted to change our school, I had very little support and absolutely no money. At first, the lack of both felt overwhelming. Now I realize that it gave me the opportunity to develop new relationships and new lines of resources.

The first time someone told me that our school could be a nationally recognized school in the National Blue Ribbon Schools Program, I actually laughed. I have learned if you can say it, you can believe it, and you can achieve it. Now, I want our students, parents, colleagues, and community to think, "Why not us?"

Hope Warrior

Chapter 10
Hope

"God will give you pieces before he gives you purpose." ~A. Clark

Amazing things began to happen when I returned from California six years ago. The first big project was getting a playground built, a project that National Insurance Company paid for. It took a year and half to get the project completed, and there were moments along the journey when I was afraid that it wasn't going to happen. That first year, I still spent a great deal of time questioning my abilities. I was still slipping back into fear. My anger was still explosive, and I really was resisting the rise; that is, allowing my ceiling to become my floor.

"I don't need to change. I don't want to change. I know the person who got me here, and she will take me the rest of the way." ~A. Clark

The true turning point came during the summer of 2013 when I was asked to start a summer program at our school to serve 150 students. The principal and board members gave me this challenge with only two weeks' notice before school ended for the summer. I had to hire staff, create a curriculum, find a food vendor, and register children. The task seemed impossible. Surely this was it, I thought. Failure was upon me.

A local leader put me in contact with a youth pastor in the community. The youth pastor agreed to try to help us launch the summer program by bringing in four high school students for four days.

All 150 students who enrolled showed up on the first day, waiting for encouraging words. I didn't have any. I felt that the situation was hopeless. The students got settled into their classrooms. I had five staff members that first year, and they were willing to try anything and everything to be successful, even though we had thirty students to a room.

Roar for Learning Summer Program students with a volunteer from Ohio in 2017

A few minutes later, the youth volunteers showed up, and there were not four of them. There were not ten volunteers. There were *fourteen* volunteers, and the next day, there were *twenty-four* volunteers. Those youth volunteers gave up their entire summers and came every single day. At end of the summer, the youth volunteers told me it was the most special school they had ever seen. They said that the way we spoke to the children was inspiring. One young woman asked if she could come back the following year, and of course, I said yes. And she did. She also came back the next year and the year after that. That young woman's name was Hope. Since 2013, hope has been the theme of my life and my work.

In 2014, I built the Hope Street Garden and Learning Lab with the help of many schools and the community of York. I tell people all the time that our community loved that garden into existence. The garden is the first of its kind. It is an outdoor learning lab for the children of York, Pennsylvania. Since then, Hope Street Garden and Learning Lab and Lincoln Charter School have hosted a thousand volunteers from all over the East Coast. Each one of those students has heard the story of Hope.

I continue to look for opportunities to improve my community and the lives of children. I worked on building a Custom Buddy Bench. I became a fellow of the

National Leadership Academy for the Public's Health. My work on Technology Tuesdays and Wellness Wednesdays was published by the National Network of Partnership Schools at Johns Hopkins University. I ran for City Council and wrote two books. I am working to complete my doctorate in public leadership.

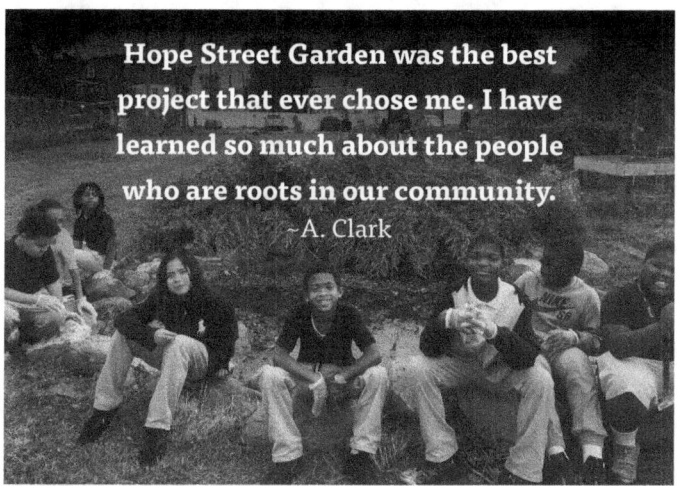

Every year, new and unbelievable rewards have come to me and to my community because I was willing to hope and work for more for our students. You hold the power to change your students' outcomes, your school, and your community by being a bringer of HOPE!

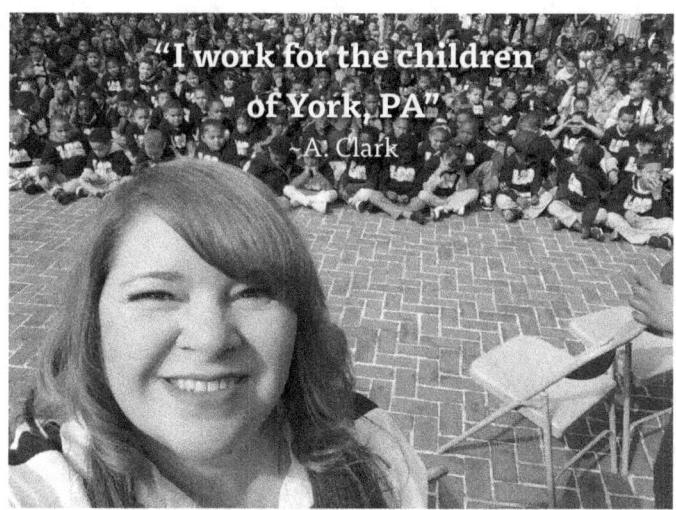

To learn more about

Anne Clark

please visit or follow her at:

Facebook
www.facebook.com/Brat1113

Facebook Messages of Hope:
www.facebook.com/groups/191665868189388

LinkedIn:
www.linkedin.com/in/anneclark13

Hope Street website:
hopestreetyorkpa.weebly.com

www.ingramcontent.com/pod-product-compliance
Lightning Source LLC
Chambersburg PA
CBHW052209110526
44591CB00012B/2146